LEARNING ADVENTURES IN READING
Grades 1–2

By the Staff of Score@Kaplan

Foreword by Alan Tripp

Simon & Schuster

**This series is dedicated to our
Score@Kaplan parents and children—
thank you for making these books possible.**

Published by
Kaplan Educational Centers and Simon & Schuster
1230 Avenue of the Americas
New York, NY 10020

Copyright © 1998 by Kaplan Educational Centers

All rights reserved. No part of this book may be reproduced or transmitted in any form or by any means, electronic or mechanical, including photocopying, recording, or by any information storage and retrieval system, without the written permission of the Publisher, except where permitted by law.

Kaplan is a registered trademark of Kaplan Educational Centers.

Special thanks to: Elissa Grayer, Doreen Beauregard, Julie Schmidt, Rebecca Geller Schwartz, Linda Lott, Janet Cassidy, Marlene Greil, Nancy McDonald, Sarah Jane Bryan, Chris Wilsdon, Janet Montal, Jeannette Sanderson, David Stienecker, Dan Greenberg, Kathy Wilmore, Dorrie Berkowitz, Brent Gallenberger, and Molly Walsh

Head Coach and General Manager, Score@Kaplan: Alan Tripp
President, Score@Kaplan: Robert L. Waldron
Series Content and Development: Mega-Books
Project Editor: Mary Pearce
Production Editor: Donna Mackay, Graphic Circle Inc.
Art Director: Elana Goren-Totino
Illustrators: Rick Brown, Ryan Brown, Sandy Forrest, Larry Nolte,
Evan Polenghi, Fred Schrier, Peter Spacek, Arnie Ten
Cover Design: Cheung Tai
Cover Photograph: Michael Britto

Manufactured in the United States of America
Published Simultaneously in Canada

January 1998
10 9 8 7 6 5 4 3 2 1

ISBN:0-684-84429-X

 # Contents

Note to Parents.. iv
Note to Kids vi

Grade One

Phonics and Spelling 1
Vocabulary.. 8
Reading Comprehension... 13
Writing... 19
Grammar, Usage, Mechanics 23
Study Skills 31

Grade Two

Phonics and Spelling 32
Vocabulary... 39
Reading Comprehension... 44
Writing... 50
Grammar, Usage, Mechanics 53
Study Skills 61

Puzzle... 64
Answers.. 65
How Do You Foster Your Child's Interest in Learning? 71

Dear Parents,

Your child's success in school is important to you, and at Score@Kaplan we are always pleased when the kids who attend our educational centers do well on their report cards. But what we really want for our kids is not just good grades. We also want everything that good grades are supposed to represent:

- We want our kids to master the key communication systems that make civilization possible: language (spoken and written), math, the visual arts, and music.
- We want them to build their critical-thinking skills so they can understand, appreciate, and improve their world.
- We want them to continually increase their knowledge and to value learning as the key to a happy, successful life.
- We want them to always do their best, to persist when challenged, to be a force for good, and to help others whenever they can.

These are ambitious goals, but our children deserve no less. We at Score@Kaplan have already helped thousands of children across the country in our centers, and we hope this series of books for children in first through sixth grades will reach many more households.

Simple Principles

We owe the remarkable success of Score@Kaplan to a few simple principles. This book was developed with these principles in mind.

- We expect every child to succeed.
- We make it possible for every child to succeed.
- We reinforce every instance of success, no matter how small.

Assessing Your Child

One helpful approach in assessing your child's skills is to ask yourself the following questions.

- How much is my child reading? At what level of difficulty?
- Has my child mastered appropriate language arts skills, such as spelling, grammar, and syntax?
- Does my child have the ability to express appropriately complex thoughts when speaking or writing?
- Does my child demonstrate mastery of all age-appropriate math skills, such as mastery of addition and subtraction facts, multiplication tables, division rules, and so on?

These questions are a good starting place and may give you new insights into your child's academic situation.

What's Going on at School

Parents will always need to monitor the situation at school and take responsibility for their child's learning. You should find out what your child should be learning at each grade level and match that against what your child actually learns.

The activity pages in *Learning Adventures* were developed using the standards developed by the professional teachers associations. As your child explores the activities in *Learning Adventures*, you might find that a particular concept hasn't been taught in school or hasn't yet been mastered by your child. This presents a great opportunity for both of you. Together you can learn something new.

Encouraging Your Child to Learn at Home

This book is full of fun learning activities you can do with your child to build understanding of key concepts in language arts, math, and science. Most activities are designed for your child to do independently. But that doesn't mean that you can't work on them together or invite your child to share the work with you. As you help your child learn, please bear in mind the following observations drawn from experience in our centers:

- Positive reinforcement is the key. Try to maintain a ratio of at least five positive remarks to every negative one.
- All praise must be genuine. Try praises such as: "That was a good try," "You got this part of it right," or "I'm proud of you for doing your best, even though it was hard."
- When a child gets stuck, giving the answer is often not the most efficient way to help. Ask open-ended questions, or rephrase the problem.
- Remember to be patient and supportive. Children need to learn that hard work pays off.

There's More to Life Than Academic Learning

Most parents recognize that academic excellence is just one of the many things they would like to ensure for their children. At Score@Kaplan, we are committed to developing the whole child. These books are designed to emphasize academic skills and critical thinking, as well as provide an opportunity for positive reinforcement and encouragement from you, the parent.

We wish you a successful and rewarding experience as you and your child embark upon this learning adventure together.

Alan Tripp
General Manager
Score@Kaplan

Dear Kids,

This is your very own book of Learning Adventures.
It has puzzles, games, riddles, and lots of other fun things for you to do.
You can do the activities alone.
Or you can share them with your family and friends.

If you get stuck on something, look for the Score coaches.
They will help you.
You can check the answers on pages 65–70, too.

We know you will do a great job.
That's why we have a special puzzle inside.
After you do three or four pages, you'll see a puzzle piece.
Cut it out.
Then glue it or tape it in place on page 64.
When you are done with the book, the puzzle will be done, too.
Then you'll find a secret message from us.

Go for it!

Your Coaches at Score

NAME_____

Oddballs

Name the pictures on each pair of cards.
Do both names begin with the same sound?
If they do, write the letter that stands for the sound.
If not, cross out the pair of cards.
The first one is done for you.

Phonics and Spelling

Review letter names and single consonant sounds

Name all the letters in the border. What sounds do the letters stand for?

Grade 1

1

Phonics and Spelling

Spell consonant sounds

NAME _____

Crack the Code

Can you crack the code?
Write the missing letter to complete each word.
Look at the bottom of the page.
Write the letter on the line above the same number.
Read the message.

Spell the words. Read the message.

1. __y__ arn

2. ___ ake

3. ___ ug

4. ___ oat

5. ___ en

6. ___ op

__y__ ou' ___ e ___ i ___ ___ ___ !
(1)   (2)   (3) (4) (5) (6)

Check Yourself: Does the message make sense? If not, try again.

2

Grade 1

NAME _____

A Tale of a Whale

Phonics and Spelling

Associate sounds with consonant digraphs and clusters

Complete each word in the story.
Use a consonant digraph or consonant cluster from the box.
Write it on the line.
Can you find other digraphs or clusters in the story?
Circle them.

| sm | cl | dr | sw | wh | dr |

A *consonant digraph* is a pair of consonants that stand for a new sound. These words begin with consonant digraphs: **th**ink, **sh**ow, **wh**ale, **ch**eer. A *consonant cluster* is a group of consonants, too. You hear the sound of each consonant in a cluster. These words begin with clusters: **sp**ring, **bl**ue, **tr**y, **st**op.

The ____cl____ouds grew dark. Then big _____ops of rain began to fall. Soon rain filled the streets. I was glad I could _____im. Then a huge _____ale floated right past my house. It gave me a big _____ile and waved its fin. The whale was holding a _____um.

"Come play with me!" it called.

Check Yourself: Did you use each digraph and cluster once? Does the story make sense?

Grade 1

3

Phonics and Spelling

Identify beginning and ending sounds of words

NAME _____

Letter Ladder

Use the clues to complete each word.
Then start at the bottom.
Read the words you made.
Can you climb all the way to the top?

Name each picture. Listen for the *beginning* sound of the picture. Name each word. Listen for the *ending* sound.

You've reached the top! You may cut out the puzzle piece now. Glue or tape the puzzle piece in place in the frame on page 64.

6. It begins like 🧦   s i ___   It ends like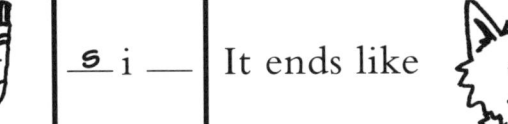

5. It begins like 🧹   ___ea ___   It ends like

4. It begins like    ___ i ___   It ends like

3. It begins like    ___ a ___   It ends like

2. It begins like    ___oa___   It ends like

1. It begins like ⌚   ___ e ___   It ends like 🦀

Around the House: Find two objects whose names begin with the same sound. Name their beginning letter. Find two more objects whose names end with the same sound. Name their ending letter.

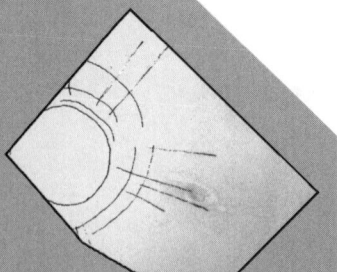

4

Grade 1

Does Your Garden Grow?

Read the word part in the middle of the flower.
Add the letter in each petal to the beginning of the word part.
Say each new word aloud.
If you made a real word, color the petal.
Write the words you make on the lines.

Phonics and Spelling

Use beginning sounds to figure out new words

sit

Phonics and Spelling

Recognize long and short vowel sounds

NAME _____

Puzzle Fun

Jane and Jan see words in this puzzle.
Can you find words that go across or down?
Write the long vowel words under Jane's name.
Write the short vowel words under Jan's name.
One is done for you.

Jane's name has a long vowel sound. Jan's name has a short vowel sound.

O	F	F	M	Q
G	A	M	E	F
O	N	S	R	E
A	T	U	L	E
T	U	N	E	T

Jane   Jan

goat _____   _____

_____   _____

_____   _____

_____   _____

_____   _____

Check Yourself: Did you find five long vowel words and five short vowel words? Good for you!

6

Grade 1

Contraction Bingo

Play contraction bingo. Here is how:
1. Toss a penny onto the word cards board. Read the two words on the card it lands on.
2. Find the contraction on the game board that stands for the two words. Make an X through it.
3. Try to get four in a row.

Phonics and Spelling

Point out and interpret contractions

A *contraction* is a way to write two words as one. Use an apostrophe (') for the missing letters.

GAME BOARD

they'll	we've	weren't	doesn't
she'll	it's	aren't	there's
wasn't	I'm	you'll	that's
he'll	let's	I've	we're

WORD CARDS

I am	we are	let us	I have
we have	are not	does not	was not
were not	he will	she will	they will
you will	it is	that is	there is

Grade 1

7

Vocabulary
Recognize and practice high-frequency words

NAME _____

Reading Race

Begin at Start.
Read each word aloud.
If you miss a word, stop reading.
Circle the word you missed.
Then go back to the beginning and start over.
Keep going until you get all the way around without stopping.

These are words you use all the time. They are called *sight* words.

Way to go! Now cut out the puzzle piece and place it in the puzzle frame on page 64.

Around the House: Have someone time you as you read the words.

Grade 1

Vocabulary
Use context clues

NAME_____

Clues in Context

Read each word.
Circle the picture it names.
Check your work by reading the sentence.
Put a check mark on the line if you were right.

First read the word.
Use the sentence meaning to check the word's meaning.

____ 1. ball
Sue tossed the ball to Abe.

____ 2. kite
The kite has a long tail.

____ 3. tree
The tree lost its leaves in the fall.

____ 4. jeep
It's fun to ride in a jeep.

____ 5. boat
The boat floats on the waves.

____ 6. horse
The horse lives in the barn.

____ 7. clown
We laughed at the clown's tricks.

____ 8. coins
I save my coins in a piggy bank.

Grade 1   9

Vocabulary

Use context clues to choose among similar words

What's the Good Word?

Read each sentence.
Find the picture that shows the meaning of the word in dark print.
Color the picture.

1. Do you like to eat **fruit** for breakfast?

2. Ray slept on a **cot** at camp.

3. An elephant has a big **trunk.**

4. I read a **book** to my little sister.

5. Dad opened a **can** of soda.

6. Mom planted a **vine** in the yard.

7. Did you hear the **phone** ring?

8. Chad went up the **stairs** to his room.

Read the whole sentence. Think about the meaning.

Around the House: Play a sentence guessing game. Say a sentence. Leave out one word. Say "blank" instead. Have someone else guess the missing word.

NAME_____

A Capital Idea

Answer each question with a proper noun. Begin each proper noun with a capital letter. Then circle the common noun in the sentence that tells what the proper noun is. One is done for you.

1. Write a good name for a new (kitten).   Puff
2. Write the name of your street._____
3. Write the name of your town or city._____
4. Write the name of your state._____
5. Write the name of your favorite store._____
6. Write the name of your teacher._____
7. Write the name of your favorite day of the week. _____
8. Write the name of the month of your birthday. _____

Check Yourself: Did you begin every answer with a capital letter?

Around the House: Make a list of the people and pets in your family. Be sure to begin each name with a capital letter.

Vocabulary

Recognize common and proper nouns

A *common noun* is the name of a person, place, or thing:
boy   elephant   city

A *proper noun* is the name of one particular person, place, or thing:
Bob   Jumbo   New York

Grade 1

Vocabulary

Learn names for months

NAME _____

Days and Dates

Look at the calendar.
Read the names of the months.
Name the holidays the pictures show.
Use the calendar to answer each question.

January	February	March	April
May	June	July	August
September	October	November	December

Every year has twelve months: January, February, March, April, May, June, July, August, September, October, November, December.

Great job! Now cut out the puzzle piece and add it to the puzzle on page 64.

1. Is Presidents' Day in February or March? _____

2. When is Halloween? _____

3. Would you say Happy New Year in January or in June? _____

4. When do you eat Thanksgiving turkey? _____

5. How many months is it from New Year's Day to Independence Day? _____

12

Grade 1

NAME _____

Tell Me Why

Look at the pictures on the page.
Then read each story.
Find the picture that tells why the story happened.
Draw a line from the picture to the story.

Reading Comprehension

Trace cause and effect in a story

a.

1. As we ran into the room, our dog growled. We were surprised. Our dog is friendly. When we talked quietly and moved slowly, she stepped aside. Then we could see what had made her act that way.

b.
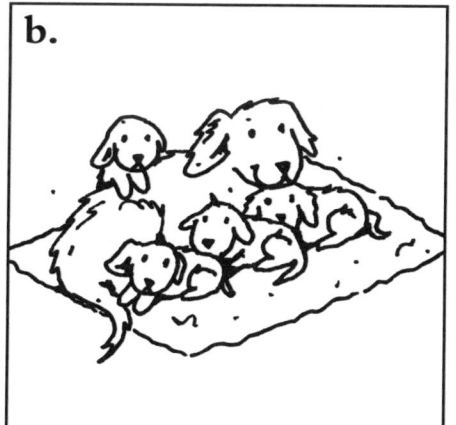

2. Zora walked into the dentist's office. She was a little worried. The dentist looked into Zora's mouth. Then she said, "I'm proud of you, Zora. You don't have any cavities!"

The *cause* tells why something happened.
The *effect* tells what happened.

Grade 1

13

Reading Comprehension

Identify beginning, middle, and end of a story

NAME _____

Map the Story

**Read each story.
Then draw pictures in the boxes to show what happened at the beginning of the story, the middle, and the end.**

Ali spotted a small cat high up in a tree. Ali knew he couldn't climb the tall tree. He called the fire department. A firefighter climbed up a tall ladder and climbed down with the kitten. He gave the kitten to Ali. Now Ali has a new pet.

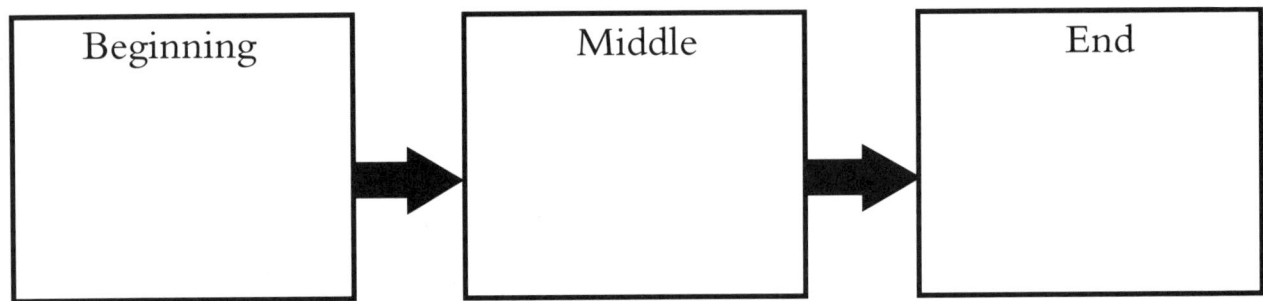

The kids on Larry's block were bored. There was no good place to play. One Saturday morning, the kids and their parents cleaned up an empty lot. The parents built benches and swings. Now Larry and the other kids play in the new park every day.

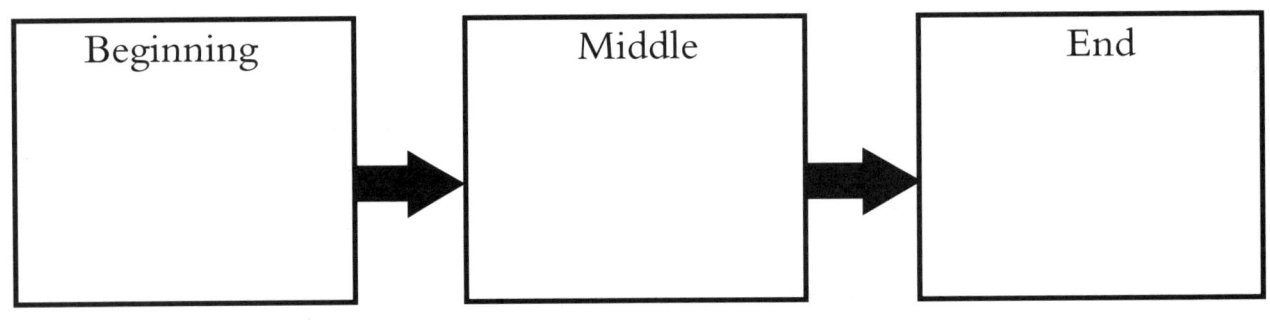

14

Grade 1

What a Dream!

**Read the story.
Use details from the story to draw a picture of the monster.**

What a Nightmare!

Last night I had a silly dream. A monster came out from under my bed. It was a big blue monster. It had one horn on the top of its head and two pointed ears. It looked at me with its three yellow eyes. I saw that its T-shirt had four armholes. That's because the monster had four arms. It opened all its arms like it wanted to give me a big hug. In my dream, I was scared. I screamed and woke up. Then I laughed. I wasn't scared any more. It was such a silly monster!

Read carefully. Take time to spot the details.

Reading Comprehension

Draw conclusions

NAME _____

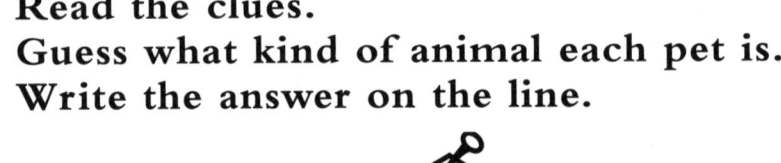

Read the clues.
Guess what kind of animal each pet is.
Write the answer on the line.

Think about animals people have for pets. Use all the clues.

Awesome! Now cut out the puzzle piece and place it on page 64.

hamster   fish   turtle   cat   dog   horse

1. Cassie has four legs.
   She has a furry coat.
   She barks when she hears a noise.
   Cassie is a
   _____.

2. Blaze has a mane.
   He is big enough for a person to sit on.
   He likes to eat oats.
   Blaze is a
   _____.

3. Maggie has four legs.
   She has a tail.
   She purrs when she is happy.
   Maggie is a
   _____.

4. Minnie swims all the time.
   She lives in a tank.
   She has fins and scales.
   Minnie is a
   _____.

Grade 1

True Blue—or Not?

The library uses blue catalogue cards for books about things that are real.
It uses yellow cards for *fantasies*.
Read each card.
If the book is about something real, color the card blue.
If it is a fantasy, color it yellow.

Fantasies are never real. They could not really happen.

1. My Dad Is from Mars
2. A Winter in Alaska
3. The Dog Who Could Do Tricks
4. The Dog Who Could Talk
5. The Tallest Building in the World
6. The Tale of the Walking Trees
7. Travel Back in Time
8. Travel in the United States

Around the House: Look at the books you have at home. Tell whether the stories are real or fantasy.

Grade 1

Reading Comprehension

Recognize fiction and nonfiction

NAME _____

A Pleasant Present

Your grandmother sent you a box of books.
Some are fiction.
Some are nonfiction.
Read each book title.
Then draw a line from each book to the shelf it belongs on.

Fiction books have stories that are made up. *Nonfiction* books tell about people, events, and ideas that are real.

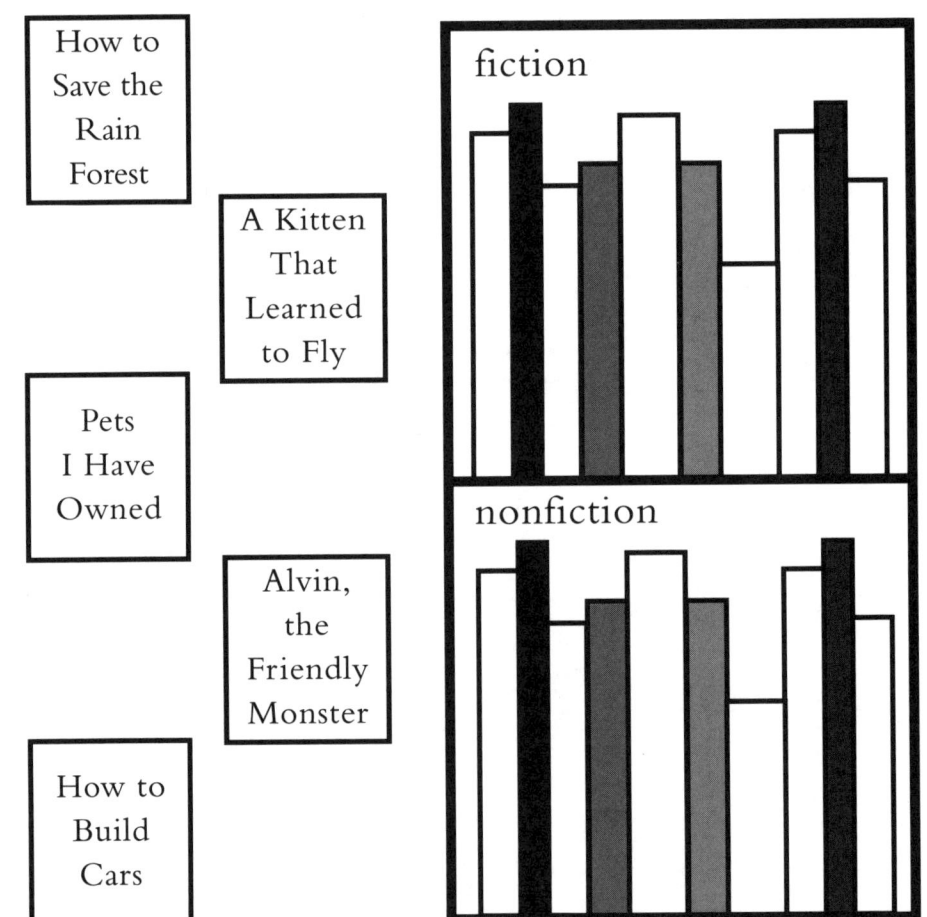

- How to Save the Rain Forest
- A Kitten That Learned to Fly
- Pets I Have Owned
- Alvin, the Friendly Monster
- How to Build Cars

Check Yourself: Read the titles of the books. Do you see a pattern? The names of these fiction books begin with vowels. The names of these nonfiction books begin with consonants.

Grade 1

NAME _____

Two Ways to Tell a Story

Writing

Put events and sentences in correct order

Look at the comic strip.
Then write the story it tells on the lines below each picture.

_____
_____
_____
_____

Be sure to write about the events in order.

_____
_____
_____
_____

Grade 1

19

Writing

Share ideas and reactions through spontaneous writing

NAME _____

Write Now!

What are you thinking?
Write your thoughts until you fill all the lines.
Write as quickly as you can.
Don't worry about spelling.
Just write what's on your mind right now.

> Close your eyes and think for a minute. Write the first idea that pops into your mind. Write about your feelings. Or write about something you did or are going to do.

> What bright ideas you have! Now cut out the puzzle piece. Find its spot in the puzzle frame on page 64 and glue or tape it in place.

Around the House: Keep a notebook handy. Once a day, stop what you are doing and fill up one page by writing your thoughts.

Writing

Think of appropriate titles for stories

NAME _____

The Name Game

Read each short story.
Think of a good title.
Write it on the line.

1. _____

Henry Ford thought cars were a great new invention. He thought every family should have one. Henry Ford found a new way to build cars so they cost less money. He called these cars Model Ts. Soon Model Ts were everywhere. All the people wanted to ride in their new Model Ts.

2. _____

We couldn't find our cat anywhere. We looked in her basket. We looked under each bed. We looked in the garage.
"Lion must have run away," Mom said sadly.
Suddenly we heard a sound in the closet. We raced to open the door. There, in a back corner, sat Lion. But Lion was not alone. Beside her were four little kittens. What a surprise!

Around the House: Go to the library with a family member. Read titles. Make a list of titles that make you want to read the book.

Before you write a title, think about the story's main idea. What is the title of your favorite book? How does the title help you know what the book is about?

Grade 1

21

Writing
Write letters and notes

NAME _____

Thanks a Lot

Read the thank-you note.
Then look at the gift in the picture.
It's for you from your Aunt Alice.
What do you think it is?
Write Aunt Alice a note to thank her for it.
Use another piece of paper if you need to.

6543 Elm Street ← **Heading**
Homeway, Indiana 00000
January 5, 2001
Greeting
Dear Grandma, **Body**
   Thank you for the new sled. It came just at the right time. It snowed hard last night, so I can use it right away. I'm on my way to the big hill now. See you soon.
Closing → Love,
Signature → Sammie

← Heading

← Greeting
← Body

Closing →

↑ Signature

22

Grade 1

NAME _____

Don't Fall In!

Read the word in each stepping stone.
Color the stones with plural words yellow.
Color the stones with singular words blue.
Then walk your fingers across the stream,
using only the yellow stones.
Don't get wet!

START

- boys
- turkey
- turtle
- sun
- dress
- kitten
- plants
- stream
- baseballs
- kangaroos
- flower
- kite
- book
- bicycle
- pigs
- doll
- beach
- boxes
- boat
- dish

FINISH

Grammar, Usage, Mechanics

Recognize singular and plural nouns

A *singular* noun names only one thing.
A *plural* noun names more than one thing. It usually ends with *s* or *es*.

Grade 1

Grammar, Usage, Mechanics

Complete sentence patterns

NAME _____

Opinion Poll

Fill in the missing part of each sentence. Write your own ideas.

Sharing your own ideas tells people what you think. It helps people get to know you better.

You may cut out the puzzle piece and place it in the puzzle frame now.

1. _____ is the best TV show.

2. My favorite game is _____.

3. _____ is a great place for a vacation.

4. _____ is a good sport to watch.

5. _____ is a good sport to play.

6. My favorite toy is a _____.

7. _____ is the best kind of pet.

8. My family is _____.

9. The tastiest snack is _____.

10. My hero is _____.

Around the House: Ask family members to complete the sentences with their own ideas.

NAME_____

Silly Sentences

Grammar, Usage, Mechanics

Distinguish declarative and interrogative sentences

Read each sentence.
If it is an asking sentence, write A on the line.
If it is a telling sentence, write T on the line.
Then match each question with an answer.
Color each sentence pair a different color.

____ Why is an island like the letter *t*?

____ Which is faster, hot or cold?

____ Why do birds fly south for the winter?

____ Why isn't your nose twelve inches long?

____ They don't have enough money to take the train.

____ How are pancakes and baseball teams alike?

____ It would be a foot.

____ They're both in the middle of *water*.

____ Hot is faster because you can catch cold.

____ They both need a good batter.

A sentence that asks a *question* is called an *asking sentence*. It ends with a question mark.
A sentence that makes a *statement* is called a *telling sentence*. It ends with a period.

Grade 1

25

Grammar, Usage, Mechanics

Recognize patterns of rhyme and repetition

NAME _____

Pattern Play

Figure out each pattern.
Then draw or write what comes next.

> Patterns have repeated parts. This is one kind of pattern: 2, 4, 2, 4. You can find patterns in pictures or wallpaper. Words can have patterns, too.

1.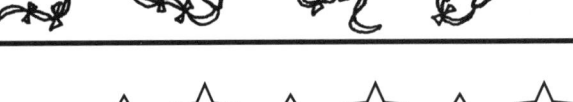
   _____

2. Old MacDonald had a farm,
   E-I-E-I-O.
   On his farm he had a cow,
   _____

3. **A**nn, **B**ob, **C**al, **D**an, **E**rnie,
   _____

4. 1, 2, 2, 2, 3, 2, 4, 2, 5, 2, _____

Grade 1

NAME _____

Tic-Tac-Toe

**In this game, you can score a tic-tac-toe by finding three vowels in a row.
The row may be across, down, or diagonal.
Find the tic-tac-toe.
Draw a straight line through it.
One is done for you.**

Grammar, Usage, Mechanics

Understand the term *vowel*

The letters *a, e, i, o,* and *u* are *vowels*. The other letters are *consonants*. Vowels *a, e, i, o,* and *u* may have either a long or a short sound.

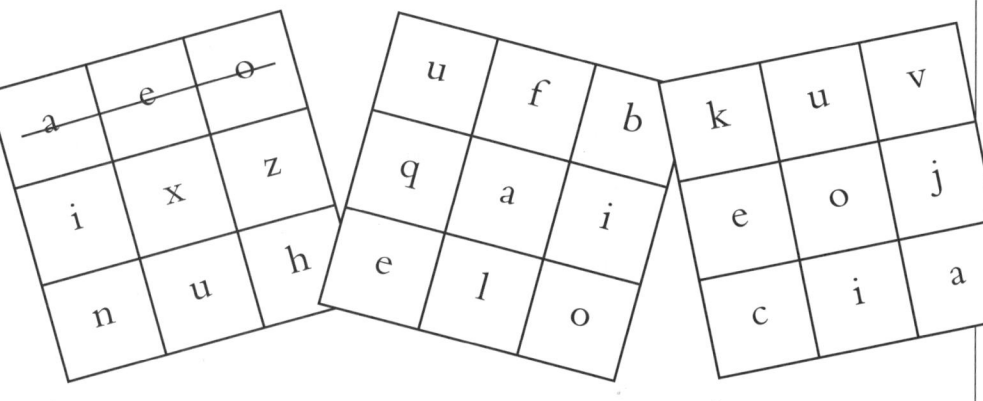

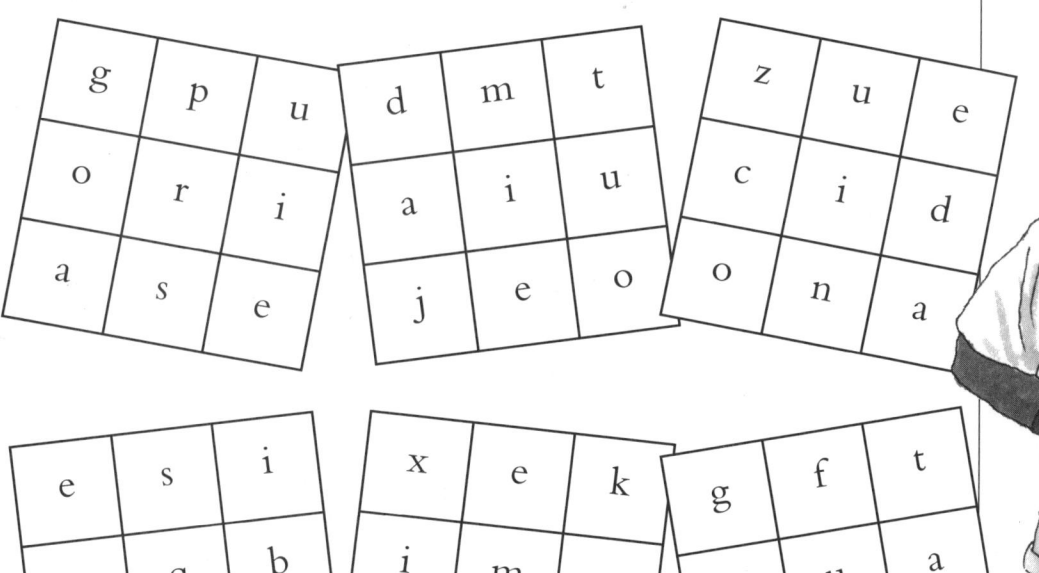

Grade 1

27

Grammar, Usage, Mechanics

Define and recognize adjectives

NAME _____

Tell Me More

Adjectives describe, or tell more about nouns. In the phrase the red rooster, the word red is the adjective.

Read each question.
Then look at the answer.
Find the adjective in the box that rhymes with the underlined noun in the answer.
Write the adjective on the line.
One is done for you.

| big | happy | ~~old~~ | strange |
| cool | loud | round | sweet |

What do you call

1. your great-grandmother's jewelry?
   Some ___old___ <u>gold</u>
2. a huge truck? A _____ <u>rig</u>
3. a fat hunting dog? A _____ <u>hound</u>
4. coins from another country?
   Some _____ <u>change</u>
5. a group of people cheering?
   A _____ <u>crowd</u>
6. an ice cream cone? A _____ <u>treat</u>
7. what you'd like to jump into on a very hot day?
   A _____ <u>pool</u>
8. your dad on the first day of vacation?
   A _____ <u>pappy</u>

That's using your head! Now cut out the puzzle piece and place it in the frame on page 64.

Grade 1

NAME_____

Let's Play

Grammar, Usage, Mechanics

Use periods and question marks to end sentences

Read the play.
Decide whether each sentence asks a question or tells something.
Write a period at the end of each telling sentence.
Write a question mark at the end of each asking sentence.

1. **Rabbit:** Turtle, why are you so slow ?
2. **Turtle:** I may be slow, but I always get there __
3. **Rabbit:** Would you run a race with me __
4. **Turtle:** I will if you want to __
5. **Rabbit:** Turtle is so far behind that I'm going to take a nap __
6. **Turtle:** Do I have a chance to win __
7. **Turtle:** I'll keep on trying anyway __
8. **Rabbit:** Where is that turtle __
9. **Rabbit:** He's so far behind I can't even see him __
10. **Turtle:** I'm not behind, Rabbit __
11. **Turtle:** Here I am in the winner's circle __
12. **Rabbit:** I can't believe I lost the race __

Around the House: Act out the play with a family member.

Listen as you read aloud these two sentences:
Did you lose your homework?
I lost my homework.
Did your voice go up when you asked the question?

Grade 1

Grammar, Usage, Mechanics

Use correct punctuation in friendly letters

NAME_____

Postcard Pals

Read each postcard.
Add the missing punctuation marks to it.

Use a *period* after a telling sentence. Use a *question mark* after a sentence that asks a question. Use a *comma* after the greeting and the closing, too.

Dear Elaine __
I'm glad you're enjoying your visit to the farm __ Here is a picture from the museum __ Do you like it __ Mom and I went there yesterday. Tomorrow we're going to the zoo __
Sincerely __
Lisa

Dear Mrs. Jackson __
My family and I are on a trip to New York City __ The buildings are really big __ Do you know which building is the tallest one in the city __ There are lots of exciting things to do here __
Sincerely __
Juan

Around the House: Get a picture postcard that shows a place near your home. Send it to someone who lives in another town.

30

Grade 1

NAME _____

Alphatown

Study Skills
Use alphabetical order

It's easy to shop in Alphatown.
All the stores are in alphabetical order.
Read each store name at the bottom of the page.
Write them in the right place in Alphatown.
One is done for you.

Say the alphabet along with me:
A, B, C, D, E,
F, G, H, I, J, K,
L, M, N, O, P,
Q, R, S, T, U,
V, W, X, Y, Z.

Alvin's Art Shop

Betty's Bakery

1. Casey's Computers

Gertie's Goods

2. _____

Lou's Lunchroom

3. _____

Paul's Pastries

4. _____

Sam's Sports Shop

5. _____

Willie's Wallets

6. _____

Zeb's Zipper Zone

Yanda's Yams   Tina's Toys   ~~Casey's Computers~~
Ned's Neckties   Hannah's Hats   Robin's Radios

Grade 1

Phonics and Spelling

Spell short and long vowel sounds

NAME _____

Dean and Dan

Dean's name has a long vowel sound. Dan's name has a short vowel sound.

Dean and Dan are twins.
Dean likes things whose names have long vowel sounds.
Dan likes things whose names have short vowel sounds.
Circle the word that completes each sentence.

1. (trucks/ trains) Dean likes to play with _____.

2. (cap/ cape) Dan likes to wear a _____.

3. (seals/ cubs) At the zoo, Dean likes to see the _____.

4. (blue/ red) Dan likes the color _____.

5. (swim/ dive) At the pool, Dean loves to _____.

6. (van/ jeep) Dan wants Mom to get a _____.

7. (drum/ flute) Dean can play the _____.

8. (sun/ snow) Dan loves days with lots of _____.

Around the House: Does your name have a long vowel sound, a short vowel sound, or both? Make a list of things that have the same kind of vowel sound as your name.

32

Grade 2

Water Wonderland

Phonics and Spelling

Learn letter-sound association for vowel pairs

NAME_____

Read the words in the box.
Find the objects in the picture.
Color each object with the color next to the object's name.

pail (yellow)	tree (brown)	toad (green)
stream (blue)	boat (red)	weeds (green)
beak (yellow)		

A vowel pair, like *ai, ea, ee,* or *oa,* usually stands for the long sound of the first vowel in the pair.

Around the House: After you've checked your answers, color the rest of the picture any way you'd like.

Grade 2

Phonics and Spelling

Spell the sounds of vowels combined with *r*

NAME _____

Riddles and Rhymes

Solve the riddles.
Use a word from the box to complete each word pair.
Write the word on the line.
The first one is done for you.

| car | park | purse | ~~fork~~ | bird | sport |

The word pairs rhyme with each other.
Here's a hint: The first word will help you spell the second one.

1. What do you call a piece of silverware for a big bird? A **stork** _fork_.
2. What do you call something you could drive in outer space? A **star** _____.
3. What do you call a bag for a hospital worker's money? A **nurse** _____.
4. What do you call the flying animal behind the first and second ones? The **third** _____.
5. What do you call a playground at night? A **dark** _____.
6. What do you call a game in the gym that just takes a minute to play? A **short** _____.

Check Yourself: Do the words in each answer rhyme? Do they end with the same word part?

34

Grade 2

NAME _____

A Fine Design

Read the words in the spaces aloud.
Listen for the syllables.
If the word has one syllable, color the space red.
If the word has two syllables, color the space yellow.
If the word has three syllables, color the space blue.

Phonics and Spelling

Apply phonics knowledge to syllables

A *syllable* is a word part that has a vowel sound. Try this trick. Touch your chin with your hand as you say a word aloud. How many times does your chin move? That's how many syllables the word has.

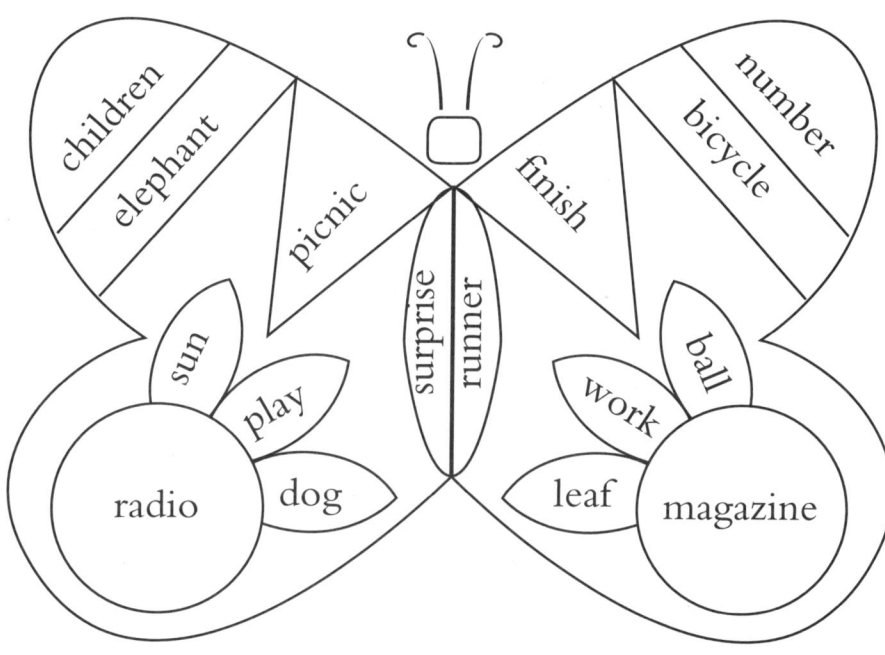

Great job! Now cut out the puzzle piece. Find its spot in the puzzle frame on page 64. Glue or tape it in place.

Check Yourself: Does your design look right to you? Are both sides the same?

Around the House: Say the names of things in your house. Listen for the number of syllables in each name. Try to find one-, two-, and three-syllable names.

Grade 2

35

Phonics and Spelling

Recognize plural endings of words

NAME _____

Count on Plurals

Do the problems.
Write the answers.
Remember to use the plural form if the answer is more than one.
The first one is done for you.

Plural means more than one. A plural noun usually ends with *s* or *es*. Add *es* to words that end with *ss*, *x*, *ch*, or *sh*. Add *s* to most other words.

1.  +  = __3__ __birds__

2. ☆☆ − ☆ = _____

3. ▢ + ▢▢▢ = _____

4.  −  = _____

5. + = _____
   (coins)

6.  −  = _____

7.  +  = _____

8.  −  = _____

Grade 2

NAME _____

Introducing—Me!

Phonics and Spelling
Write numbers and letters

Practice writing letters and numbers on another sheet of lined paper.
Then use your best handwriting to answer the questions.

```
Aa  Bb  Cc  Dd  Ee  Ff  Gg  Hh  Ii
Jj  Kk  Ll  Mm  Nn  Oo  Pp  Qq  Rr
Ss  Tt  Uu  Vv  Ww  Xx  Yy  Zz
     1 2 3 4 5 6 7 8 9 10
```

1. What is your first name? _____
2. What is your middle name? _____
3. What is your last name? _____
4. How old are you? _____
5. What is your telephone number? _____
6. What is your address? _____
   _____
7. What is your favorite TV show? _____
   _____
8. What is your favorite book? _____
   _____
9. What is your favorite game? _____
   _____

Grade 2

Phonics and Spelling

Begin to proofread for correct spelling

NAME _____

News You Can Use

Read the newspaper headlines.
Find the misspelled word in each sentence.
Circle the word.
Then write it correctly on the line.

NEWS
Second grade takes trip to the zo. _____

NEWS
Dwayne wins art priz. _____

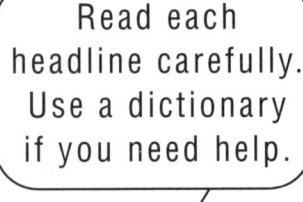
Read each headline carefully. Use a dictionary if you need help.

NEWS
Ran spoils class picnic. _____

NEWS
First graid puts on play. _____

NEWS
Enter the speling bee. _____

NEWS
Sue reads a dook a day. _____

Around the House: Write a headline about something special you did with your family.

38

Grade 2

NAME_____

Vocabulary

Recognize words with several meanings

Riddle Riot

Read each riddle.
Find the word in the box that fits the clues.
Write the word on the line.
One is done for you.

| foot | bat | scale | ~~run~~ |
| head | fan | bank | ruler |

Some words have more than one meaning. Which word fits both the clues in each riddle?

1. You can score one in a baseball game or do this in a race. What is it? __run__
2. This is the leader of a group or something that sits on top of your neck. What is it? _____
3. You can keep money in it or find one beside a river. What is it? _____
4. It is the body part at the end of your leg or a length of twelve inches. What is it? _____
5. It is a small animal that flies at night or a stick you use to hit a ball. What is it? _____
6. It is the leader of a country or a stick you measure with. What is it? _____
7. It is the covering on a fish or something you use to weigh yourself. What is it? _____
8. It is a machine that keeps you cool or a person who really likes something. What is it? _____

Way to go! You're a pro! Cut out the puzzle piece and put it in the right spot on page 64.

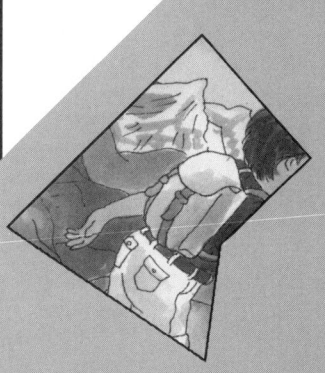

Grade 2

Vocabulary
Give synonyms and antonyms

NAME _____

Blast Off!

Synonyms are words that have the same meaning, such as big and large. *Antonyms* are opposites, such as big and little.

Read the words in the middle column. Choose a synonym and an antonym from the box for each word. Write them where they belong. The first one is done for you.

big	small	mean	ugly	clean	beautiful
go	easy	hard	chilly	kind	glad
stay	hot	whisper	sad	shout	filthy

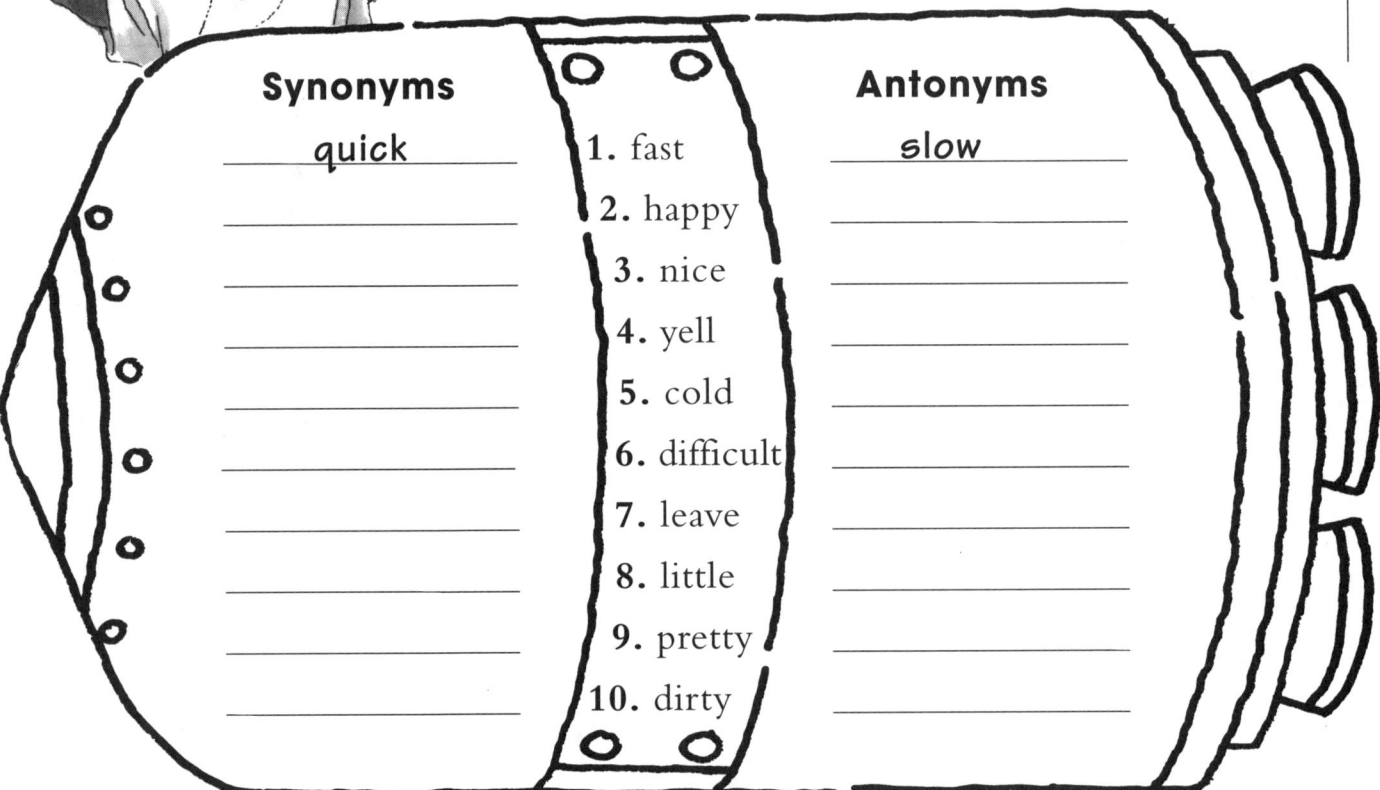

Synonyms

quick

Antonyms

slow

1. fast
2. happy
3. nice
4. yell
5. cold
6. difficult
7. leave
8. little
9. pretty
10. dirty

40

Grade 2

High Score

Look at the word box.
Pick one word from each column to make a compound word.
Write the compound word in a basketball.
Make as many words as you can.
Then give yourself two points for each word.

back	pack
ball	pan
bow	pea
box	rain
cake	sand
end	self
flake	foot
side	snow
my	walk
nut	week

Compound words are made from two smaller words. Here are some compound words: *basketball, popcorn, wheelchair.*

Your Score _____

Vocabulary
Use sound words and sensory words

NAME _____

Common Senses

Read the words in the box.
Write each word under the sense the word tells about.

bitter	crash	loud	salty	sunny
blue	dark	musty	scream	sweet
bright	stinky	perfumed	smoky	wet
cool	hot	prickly	sour	purr

Sight	Sound	Touch	Taste	Smell

Most people have five senses. We can see, hear, smell, feel, and taste. Each sense tells us something different.

Around the House: Sit quietly for a few minutes. Listen to the sounds around you. Then list all the things you heard.

42

Grade 2

NAME_____

Sounds and Sentences

Vocabulary
Use vowel or consonant patterns to choose between similar words

Name the two pictures.
Then read the sentence.
Circle the picture that shows the meaning of the word in dark print.

1.  Would you like to sit on the **chair**?

2.   I saw a **bee** in the back yard.

3.   Artie cleaned up the spill with an old **mop**.

4.   The **hen** pecked at the grain.

5.   The **frog** jumped into the pond.

6.   Do you hear the **crow** in the field?

7. 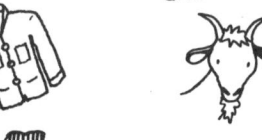 The fuzzy **goat** feels soft.

8.  Jen made a puppet from a **sock**.

Some words sound almost alike. Don't be fooled!

Good for you! Go ahead and cut out the puzzle piece. Add it to the puzzle on page 64.

Around the House: Play a sentence guessing game. Say a sentence. Leave out one word. Say "blank" instead. Have someone else guess the missing word.

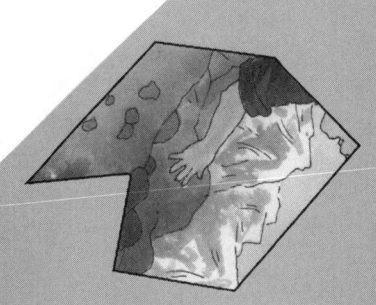

Reading Comprehension

Follow plot sequence in a story

NAME _____

Which Came First?

Read each part of the story. Then number the sentences to show the order that things happened.

Each thing that happens in a story is called an *event*. The order of the events tells what happens first, second, third, and so on.

Today was our all-school Olympics. Right after the bell rang, we all went outdoors. In the morning we had races. There were hopping races, sack races, and running races. We were thirsty after the races, so we had a break and drank juice.

_____ a. The children ran races.

_____ b. The bell rang.

_____ c. Everyone went outdoors.

_____ d. Everyone took a juice break.

After our break, we played class tug of war. By then, it was time for lunch. In the afternoon, we played baseball. At the end of the day, the principal gave out prizes. Guess what! I won a blue ribbon.

_____ e. The principal gave out prizes.

_____ f. The children ate lunch.

_____ g. Everyone played baseball.

_____ h. The children played tug of war.

Check Yourself: Read the sentences in number order. Do your sentences and the paragraphs tell the same story?

Who's Who?

Cindy and Sandy are best friends.
But they are very different.
Read about the two characters.
Then answer the questions.

Cindy is nice, but she's quiet and shy. She likes to read and play quiet games. She is very good at math.

Sandy is nice, too. She talks a lot and is friendly. She likes to keep moving. She is a good artist.

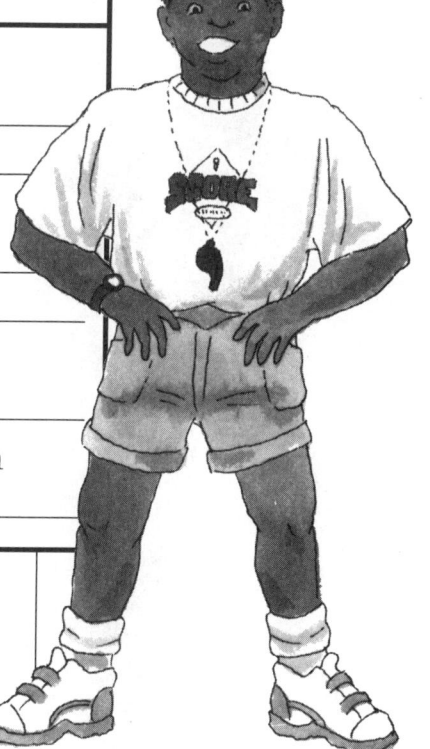

Think about what you know about Cindy and Sandy. Decide how you think they will act.

1. When the girls play together, who wants to jump rope? _____
2. Who wants to play a computer game? _____
3. When the girls go shopping, who figures out that they got the wrong change? _____
4. Who tells the clerk about it? _____
5. When the girls meet a new friend, who talks first? _____
6. When the girls play inside on a rainy day, who can think of good things to do? _____

Around the House: Write about yourself. Tell what you are like.

Reading Comprehension
Understand characters' motivations

Grade 2

Reading Comprehension

Recognize different types of literature

NAME _____

You Be the Judge

Your class has saved its best writing all year.
Read each piece of writing.
Write *poetry* or *fable* on the line to show what kind of writing each piece is.

A *fable* is a kind of short story. It teaches a lesson, such as "Many helpers make work easy." *Poetry* has short lines. It usually has a rhythm and some rhyming words.

○ _____
I Like Beets
A big red beet
Is quite a treat.
It tastes so sweet.

○ _____
The Empty Pool
Every morning Dog jumped into the pool without looking.
"Dog," Cat said, "you should never jump into water without looking to see how deep it is."
"It's always the same," Dog said.
When fall came, the owners drained the pool. Dog ran out and jumped in the pool. Then Dog climbed out the pool, dizzy and hurt.
"I told you so," said Cat.
Lesson: Look before you leap.

What's the Story?

Read the story.
Use a pencil to draw a picture.
Show the setting and the characters.
Then use crayons to color the character who is telling the story.

Slinky Snake Makes Friends

A snake's life can be lonely. I know, because I'm a snake. My friends call me Slinky. Now that I have friends, that is. Not long ago, the animals by my pond wouldn't play with me.

One day I was sunning myself on a rock by the pond. I heard a squeak. Milo Mouse had fallen into the pond.

"Help!" Milo shouted. "I can't swim."

Quick as a wink, I slithered off my rock. I wrapped my tail around a thick weed. Then I stretched myself out, stiff as a board.

"Climb on," I hissed. "Use me as a bridge."

Milo was still afraid. He thought he was going to drown or be eaten by a snake. Finally he got so cold and wet, he had to jump on and run across my back.

"Slinky," he said, "you're not scary at all. You're not even slimy. Let's be friends."

Now all the animals are my friends. They know I won't hurt them.

The *setting* is the place where the story happens. The *characters* are the people or animals in the story.

Reading Comprehension

Appreciate rhyme and rhythm

NAME _____

Silly Rhymes

Words that rhyme have the same ending sound, even when they are not spelled the same way. These words rhyme: *true/new* and *said/bed*. The lines of a poem don't always rhyme with each other.

Read each poem.
Clap along as you read.
Then read the last word in each line again.
Circle the words that rhyme.

1. **Mary Had a Little Lamb**
   Mary had a little lamb.
   Its fleece was white as snow.
   And everywhere that Mary went
   The lamb was sure to go.

2. **Mary's Goat**
   When the lamb ran away
   Mary got a goat.
   Mary gave her goat some hay
   And a nice new coat.

3. **You in the Zoo**
   What would you do
   If you lived in the zoo
   And shared a big cage
   With a blue kangaroo?

4. **A Meal for a Queen**
   Succotash, pot roast,
   Or lettuce that's green—
   Which food do you think
   Is fit for a queen?

48

Grade 2

Tangle Your Tongue

Reading Comprehension
Understand and appreciate alliteration

Read the tongue twisters aloud. Practice until you can read them quickly.

Ten tiny tots tossed twenty twinkling toys.
Shelly showed shy Sherry how she should shovel.

Then unscramble the mixed up words in each sentence below to make new tongue twisters. The words are in the box.

In a tongue twister, most of the words begin with the same sound.

| Happy | buns | Can | canes | baked |
| wishes | Which | home | carry | hit |

1. _____ witch whispered her three _____ ?
   ihwhc   *sihwse*

2. Betty _____ billions of _____ in Benny's bakery.
         akbed   *nubs*

3. _____ Harry _____ a hundred _____ runs.
   pahpy   *ith*   *meho*

4. _____ Ken _____ candy _____ to Canada?
   acn   *yrrac*   *necas*

Around the House: Make up your own tongue twister. Practice until you can say it quickly. Then challenge a family member to repeat it.

Grade 2

49

Writing
Follow a pattern to write sentences

NAME _____

Sentence Scramble

Choose a word or phrase from each column to make a sentence.
Write it on the line.
Make five sentences all together.

Who or What?	What Happened?	How, When, or Where?
The sunflower	sings	every afternoon.
A little frog	were turning	into the pond.
My friend and I	jog	around and around.
My dad	hopped	quickly.
The wheels	grew	in the shower.

1. _____
2. _____
3. _____
4. _____
5. _____

This sentence has three parts:
The puppies/
played/
in the mud.
The first part tells who or what the sentence is about. The second part tells what happened. The third part tells how, when, or where it happened.

Around the House: Play a game. Say the beginning of a sentence. Then work with family members to add as many different endings as you can.

Grade 2

Writing
Use exact words

NAME_____

Picture This

Make the circus poster more exciting. Replace each underlined word with a word from the tent shape.

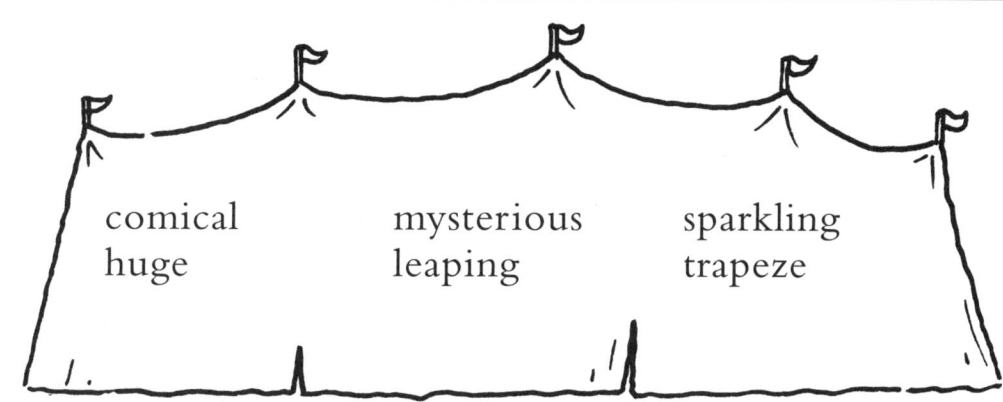

comical   mysterious   sparkling
huge   leaping   trapeze

1. Come see the <u>big</u> elephant.
   _____

2. See some <u>good</u> magic tricks.
   _____

3. Watch lions <u>going</u> through hoops.
   _____

4. Laugh at the <u>funny</u> clowns.
   _____

5. See acrobats fly through the air on a <u>thing</u>. _____

6. Let yourself be dazzled by the <u>pretty</u> costumes. _____

Some words don't really tell you very much at all. Exact words help you make a picture in your mind. The phrase *a nice day* doesn't tell you much. The phrase *a sunny day* helps you form a picture.

You may cut out the puzzle piece now. Glue or tape the puzzle piece in place in the frame on page 64. Do you think you know what the picture is yet?

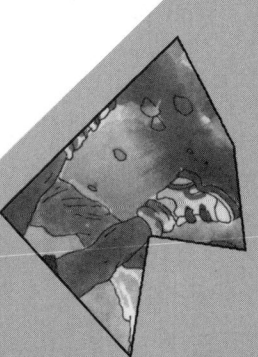

Grade 2   **51**

Writing
Write stories and descriptions

NAME _____

Setting and Story

Look carefully at the picture.
Write sentences to describe it on the lines below.
Then write a story about something that could happen in the picture.
Use another sheet of paper for your story.

A *description* tells how something looks, sounds, feels, smells, or tastes.
A *story* has action and events.

Grade 2

NAME _____

Lights! Camera! Action!

Grammar, Usage, Mechanics

Define verb and identify action verbs

Read each sentence.
Unscramble the word in dark print to find the verb.
Write the verb on the line.

A *verb* is a word that shows action, like *run* or *play*. An action can happen without showing movement. It can be something that happens in your mind, like *read* or *think*.

_____ 1. Katie and Karen **pmuj** rope.

_____ 2. We **lawk** to school every day.

_____ 3. Mom and Dad **ojg** on Sundays.

_____ 4. Joe and Dave always **tae** lunch at noon.

_____ 5. Then they **ader** books for a while.

_____ 6. Sometimes they **snig** songs.

_____ 7. My friend and I often **ktla** on the phone.

_____ 8. I **tiwer** a letter to Grandma once a week.

_____ 9. We **miws** at the city pool.

_____ 10. Our little sisters **phalss** around in the baby pool.

Check Yourself: Did you use all the letters in each word? Does every word you wrote name an action?

Around the House: Go to a place where it's okay to move around. Act out each of the verbs you wrote.

Grade 2

Mystery Picture

Find the hidden picture.
Read each sentence.
Is the verb used correctly in the sentence?
If it is, color the space yellow.

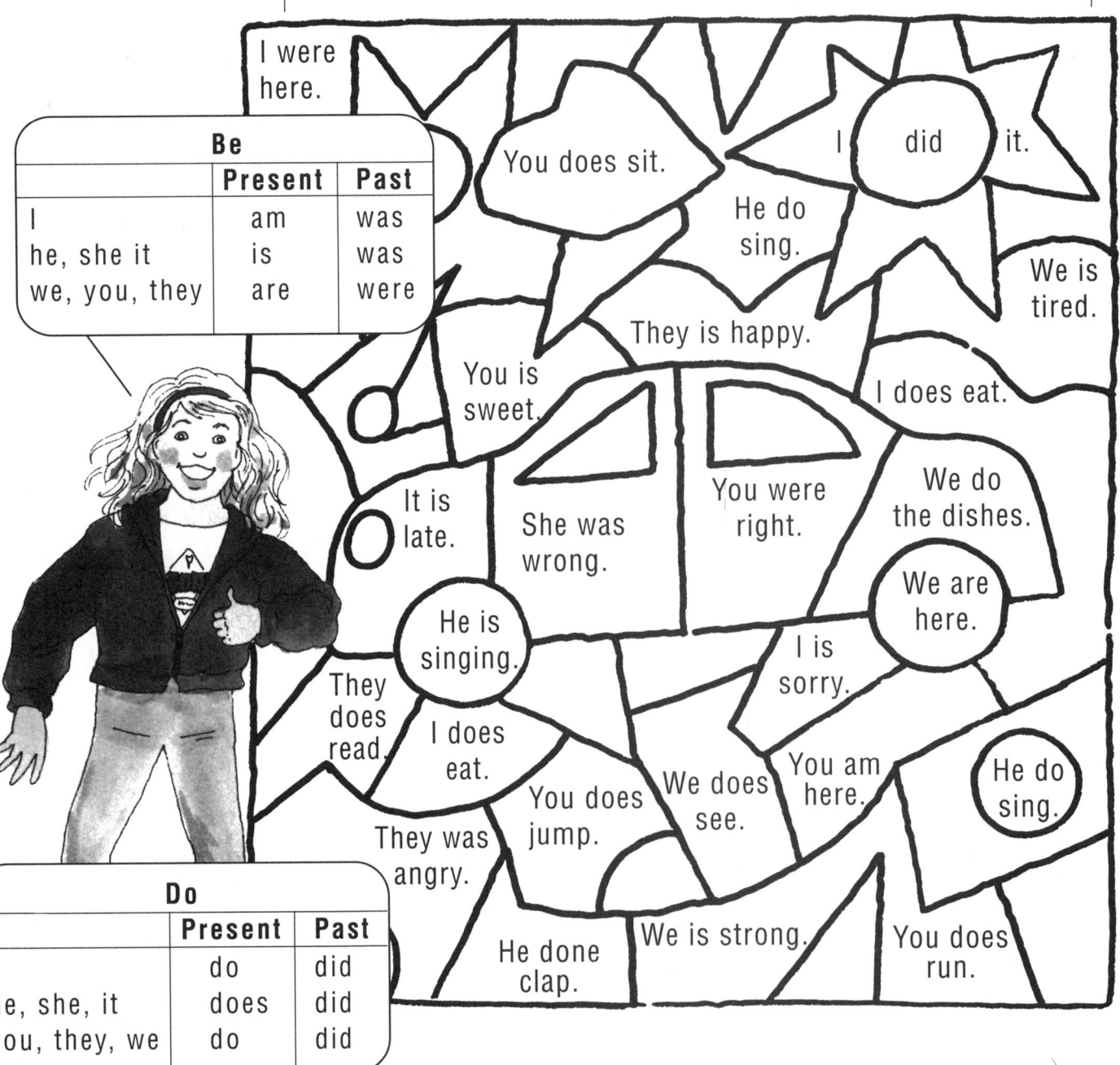

NAME_____

Get Set, Go!

Grammar, Usage, Mechanics

Learn present and past tenses of regular verbs

The two racers below are running a race. If they can run the whole four miles, they are winners. Help them win.
Read the underlined verb in each sentence. Circle Present or Past.
Then check your work. Score one mile for each one you did correctly.

The verb in this sentence is in *present tense*: My pal and I <u>talk</u> on the phone. The verb in this sentence is in the *past tense:* I <u>talked</u> to my friend yesterday.

1. Arlene <u>jumps</u> rope every day.
   Present   Past
2. Mom already <u>fixed</u> the broken toy.
   Present   Past
3. After our homework is done, we <u>watch</u> TV.
   Present   Past
4. Our snowman <u>melted</u> yesterday.
   Present   Past

Score:_____

5. Last Tuesday it <u>rained</u> all day.
   Present   Past
6. Tyrone <u>needs</u> new shoes.
   Present   Past
7. I <u>hope</u> we can go to the zoo.
   Present   Past
8. Sam <u>laughed</u> at Tony's joke.
   Present   Past

Score:_____

Good for you! Go ahead and cut out the puzzle piece and add it to the puzzle on page 64.

Check Yourself: Did you circle Past for all the verbs that end in *ed*?

Grade 2

Grammar, Usage, Mechanics

Recognize and compare adjectives

NAME _____

Adjective Game

Read each sentence below.
Underline the adjective.
Does the adjective compare two things?
If it does, color the rectangle red.
If it doesn't, color the rectangle yellow.

An adjective that ends with *er* compares two things. Read this sentence: Grandpa's truck is bigger than his friend's truck. The adjective *bigger* helps you compare two trucks.

1. There are three trees in my yard.	**5.** The lake has deeper water than the river.
2. Is Jake a faster runner than you?	**6.** A kangaroo is taller than a mouse.
3. I like the yellow bike.	**7.** Katie has a little kitten.
4. The daisy is a pretty flower.	**8.** Kenny has a bigger cat than I have.

Grammar, Usage, Mechanics

Understand verb tenses

Do You Agree?

Read each sentence.
Circle the correct verb form for each one.

1. Leatha (sit, sits) beside me on the bus.

2. Tran and Ron (play, plays) baseball at recess.

3. The puppies (sleep, sleeps) most of the time.

4. My big brother (ride, rides) his bike to school.

5. Mom (work, works) at the hospital.

6. Matt (wait, waited) for me after school.

7. Sue (call, called) Chris on the phone.

8. Luisa (want, wanted) a new pair of shoes.

9. Jerome (ask, asked) Omar to come to the party.

10. Afi (need, needed) to sharpen her pencil.

If the subject is just one person or thing, add *s* to the verb.
A *present tense* verb tells about something that is happening now. A *past tense* verb tells about something that happened in the past.

Grammar, Usage, Mechanics
Understand contractions

Contraction Crossword

Read the two words for each clue.
Put them together to make a contraction.
Write the contraction in the puzzle.
The apostrophes are already in place.
One is done for you.

Remember that a *contraction* is one word that stands for two, like this: it's = it is. Every contraction has an *apostrophe* to show which letters were left out.

ACROSS
2. Could not
5. Will not
6. I have
7. She is
8. I am
9. Do not

DOWN
1. You have
3. They are
4. Does not
8. I would

58

Grade 2

Know the Score

Read each sentence.
Find each small letter that should be capitalized.
Cross it out, and write the capital letter above it.
Write the number of mistakes in the sentence on the line.

_____ 1. our family doctor is named dr. Valentine.

_____ 2. I have a dog named Maggie and a cat named cassie.

_____ 3. allen smith was born in indiana.

_____ 4. My teacher is mr. purdy.

_____ 5. everyone at memorial School was in the talent show.

_____ 6. we went to boston, massachusetts, for vacation.

_____ 7. Erin's favorite holiday is thanksgiving.

_____ 8. turn left at main street.

SCORE BOARD	
Home	Visitors
	15

Check Yourself: When you finish, add the numbers. Write your number on the score board. If you found all the mistakes, your score will add up to 17.

Remember to begin every sentence with a capital letter. Capitalize proper nouns, too, and titles like Dr., Ms., or Mr.

Grammar, Usage, Mechanics
Understand capitalization

Grammar, Usage, Mechanics

Learn use of commas

NAME _____

Commas Count

Today you're the teacher.
Write in the missing commas.
Then give a grade.
Give a ✗ for 1 missing comma.
Give a ☹ for 2 missing commas.
Give a ✓ for 3 missing commas.
Draw a ☆ on the perfect paper.

When you write a letter, use a comma between the city and state in your address. Place a comma before the year in the date. And don't forget the comma after the letter's greeting.

○ 20 Royalton Place, Apt. 2
Sunnytown California 90200
July 10 2000

Dear Kathy,
I'm glad you like your new school. I miss you, though.

○ 324 River Road
Big River, Texas 71000
September 30, 1998

Dear Brian,
Guess what! Our team won our first game.

○ 2513 Lake Avenue
Mirror Lake Alabama 35000
April 7 1999

Dear Artie
Thanks for inviting me to visit you last week. I really had fun.

○ 6543 Tulip Trail
Washington, Kentucky 42000
August 29, 2001

Dear Mary
○ I'm so happy that you want to be pen pals. We'll learn a lot about each other and our countries.

60

Grade 2

Study Skills
Use guide words

NAME _____

Look It Up

Help write a dictionary.
Read each set of guide words and definitions.
Find the word from the box that belongs with each one.
Write it on the line.
One is done for you.

| jingle | bronco | ~~broccoli~~ | farm | pigsty |
| easel | fast | picnic | ebony | jockey |

1. bring/brother
broccoli A green vegetable with a round head on a stalk.
_____ A wild horse.

2. earthquake/editor
_____ A stand for a painting.
_____ A deep black color.

3. family/favor
_____ Land used to raise animals and grow crops.
_____ Moving very quickly.

4. jewel/joke
_____ A soft ringing sound.
_____ A person who rides a horse in a race.

5. piano/pilot
_____ An outdoor meal.
_____ A place where pigs are kept.

Entry words in a dictionary are in alphabetical order. Each entry word has a definition. *Dictionary guide words* show the first and last word on each page.

Grade 2

Study Skills
Identify the parts of a book

NAME _____

Be a Bookworm

There are different places in a book to look for information.
Read about the different places below.
Then follow the directions on the next page.

Hmm... I wonder what information is in this book. Just look in the table of contents.

You're almost there! You know what to do with your puzzle piece.

The title page includes the book title, author, and publisher.

The table of contents lists what you will find in the book.

It has chapter names and page numbers.

The glossary gives the meanings of hard words.

The index lists topics and their page numbers.

It is in alphabetical order.

Around the House: Look in your library books to find the title page, table of contents, glossary, and index.

Grade 2

NAME _____

Study Skills
Identify the parts of a book

Can you identify each book part below? Write *title page, table of contents, glossary,* or *index* on the line.

---

astronaut a person who flies into space
colony a new settlement in a faraway place
launch a space ship's blast off
mission a trip taken for a special purpose

1. _____

Flying into Space
by
Pam Smith
Readers' Favorites, Inc.

2. _____

Introduction 3
The First
Space Ships 9
The Apollo
Astronauts 17
Can We Live
in Space? 23

3. _____

Cosmonaut 18-19
Halley's Comet 7
Mars 22, 25
Sputnik 4

4. _____

Great work! Now find the right spot for your final puzzle piece on page 64. Congratulations!

Grade 2

63

Puzzle

Here's where you glue or paste the puzzle pieces you cut out. When you put them all in place, you'll see your secret message.

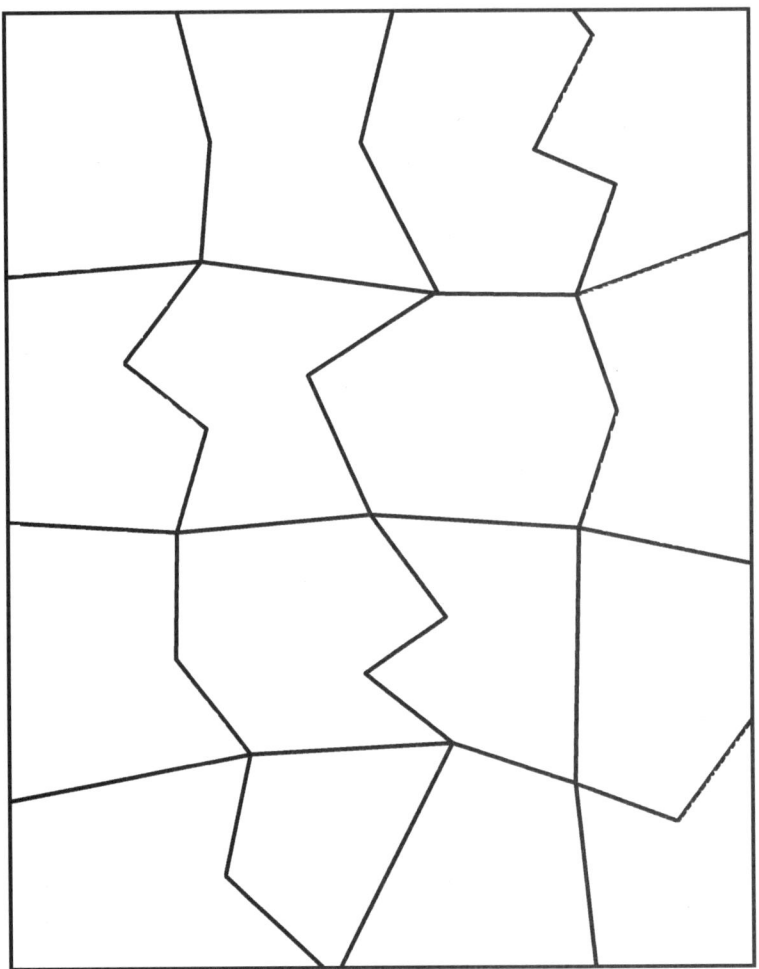

Grades 1 & 2

Answers

Page 1
2. s
3. v
4. n
5. d
6. cross out

Page 2
2. r
3. r
4. g
5. h
6. t
You're right!

Page 3
drops
swim
whale
smile
drum
Other diagraphs: the, then.
Other clusters: grew, streets, glad, floated, play.

Page 4
6. six
5. meal
4. zip
3. van
2. goat
1. web

Page 5
sit, bit, kit, hit
hen, ten, men, pen
hug, rug, tug, bug
hop, mop, top, pop
had, dad, bad, sad

Page 6

Jane	Jan
goat	fan
game	sun
tune	ant
feet	off
oat	net

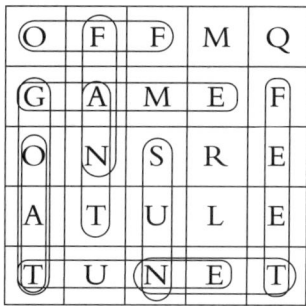

Page 7
Answers will vary.

Page 8
Answers will vary.

Page 9
1. (baseball)
2. (kite)
3. (tree)
4. (jeep)
5. (sailboat)
6. (horse)
7. (sheep)
8. (coins)

Page 10
1. (fruit)
2. (bed)
3. (elephant)
4. (book)
5. (can)
6. (vine)
7. (telephone)
8. (stairs)

Page 11
Answers will vary, but each answer should begin with a capital letter.

Grades 1 & 2

Page 12
1. February
2. October
3. January
4. November
5. Six months

Page 13
1. b
2. a

Page 14
Answers will vary.

Page 15
Picture should show a blue monster with a horn on the top of its head, three yellow eyes, and four arms. It should be wearing a T-shirt.

Page 16
1. dog
2. horse
3. cat
4. fish

Page 17
1. yellow
2. blue
3. blue
4. yellow
5. blue
6. yellow
7. yellow
8. blue

Page 18
Fiction titles: A Kitten That Learned to Fly; Alvin, the Friendly Monster
Nonfiction titles: How to Save the Rain Forest, Pets I Have Owned, How to Build Cars

Page 19
Sample answer:
Pat was rowing the boat. Then along came Vic. "Can I ride, too?" Vic called. Pat rowed to the dock, and Vic climbed in. Then Maggie came along. "Woof! Woof!" Maggie barked. "Wait for me!" Bump! Splash! Maggie was in the boat. Then all of a sudden, no one was in the boat. Maggie had tipped it over. "Bad dog," yelled Pat and Vic angrily. "This is fun!" barked Maggie.

Page 20
Answers will vary.

Page 21
Sample answers:
1. A Good Idea
2. Kitten Surprise

Page 22
Answers will vary, but should include all five letter parts, the phrase "thank you," the robot, and a mention of how it will be used.

Page 23
Yellow (plural):
boys
plants
baseballs
kangaroos
pigs
boxes

Blue (singular):
turkey	kite
turtle	book
dress	doll
sun	beach
kitten	boat
stream	dish
flower	
bicycle	

Page 24
Answers will vary.

Page 25
Sentence pairs:
1. How are pancakes and baseball teams alike? A
   They both need a good batter. T
2. Why is an island like the letter *t*? A
   They're both in the middle of *water*. T
3. Which is faster, hot or cold? A
   Hot is faster because you can catch cold. T
4. Why do birds fly south for the winter? A
   They don't have enough money to take the train. T
5. Why isn't your nose twelve inches long? A
   It would be a foot. T

Page 26
1. △
2. E-I-E-I-O
3. Any name that begins with **F**
4. 6, 2

Page 27

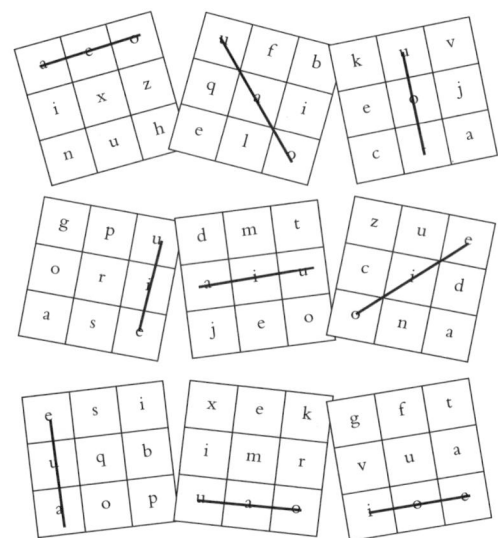

Page 28
2. big
3. round
4. strange
5. loud
6. sweet
7. cool
8. happy

Page 29
2. period
3. question mark
4. period
5. period
6. question mark
7. period
8. question mark
9. period
10. period
11. period
12. period

Page 30

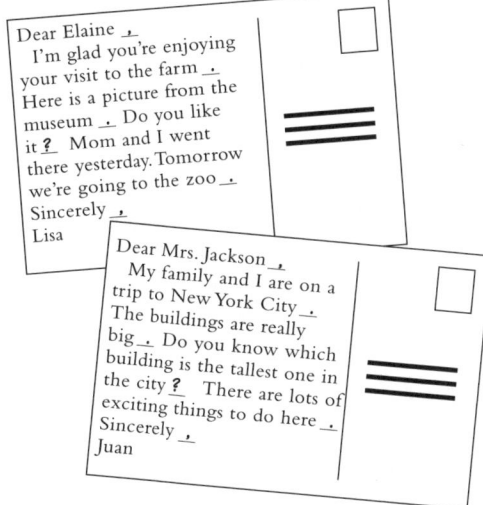

Page 31
2. Hannah's Hats
3. Ned's Neckties
4. Robin's Radios
5. Tina's Toys
6. Yanda's Yams

Page 32
1. trains
2. cap
3. seals
4. red
5. dive
6. van
7. flute
8. sun

Page 33
yellow: pail, beak
green: toad, weeds
brown: tree
blue: stream
red: boat

Page 34
2. car
3. purse
4. bird
5. park
6. sport

Grades 1 & 2

Page 35
red: sun, play, dog, ball, work, leaf
yellow: surprise, runner, children, number, picnic, finish
blue: bicycle, radio, magazine, elephant

Page 36
2. 1 star
3. 4 boxes
4. 1 boy
5. 5 dimes
6. 2 glasses
7. 6 watches
8. 4 mules

Page 37
Answers will vary.

Page 38
1. zoo
2. prize
3. Rain
4. grade
5. spelling
6. book

Page 39
2. head
3. bank
4. foot
5. bat
6. ruler
7. scale
8. fan

Page 40
2. glad/sad
3. kind/mean
4. shout/whisper
5. chilly/hot
6. hard/easy
7. go/stay
8. small/big
9. beautiful/ugly
10. filthy/clean

Page 41
Sample answers: backpack, football, rainbow, sandbox, pancake, weekend, snowflake, myself, peanut, sidewalk

Page 42
1. **Sight:** blue, bright, dark, sunny
2. **Sound:** crash, loud, scream, purr
3. **Touch:** cool, hot, prickly, wet
4. **Taste:** bitter, salty, sour, sweet
5. **Smell:** musty, stinky, perfumed, smoky

Page 43
1. chair
2. bee
3. broom
4. chicken
5. frog
6. crow
7. goat
8. sock

Page 44
a. 3
b. 1
c. 2
d. 4
e. 8
f. 6
g. 7
h. 5

Page 45
1. Sandy
2. Cindy
3. Cindy
4. Sandy
5. Sandy
6. Cindy

Page 46
1. poem
2. fable

Page 47
Children's pictures should show the edge of a pond, surrounded by weeds and rocks. The animal characters should include a snake and a mouse. Only the snake should be colored in.

Page 48
1. snow/go
2. away/hay, goat/coat
3. do/zoo/kangaroo/blue
4. green/queen

Page 49
1. Which, wishes
2. baked, buns
3. Happy, hit, home
4. Can, carry, canes

Page 50
Possible answers:
1. The sunflower grew quickly.
2. A little frog hopped into the pond.
3. My best friend and I jog every afternoon.
4. My dad sings in the shower.
5. The wheels were turning around and around.

Page 51
1. huge
2. mysterious
3. leaping
4. comical
5. trapeze
6. sparkling

Page 52
Answers will vary. The description should include details from the picture, but no story action. The story should have a plot.

Page 53
1. jump
2. walk
3. jog
4. eat or ate
5. read
6. sing
7. talk
8. write
9. swim
10. splash

Page 54

Page 55
1. Present
2. Past
3. Present
4. Past
5. Past
6. Present
7. Present
8. Past

Page 56
1. yellow—three
2. red—faster
3. yellow—yellow
4. yellow—pretty
5. red—deeper
6. red—taller
7. yellow—little
8. red—bigger

Page 57
1. sits
2. play
3. sleep
4. rides
5. works
6. waited
7. called
8. wanted
9. asked
10. needed

Page 58

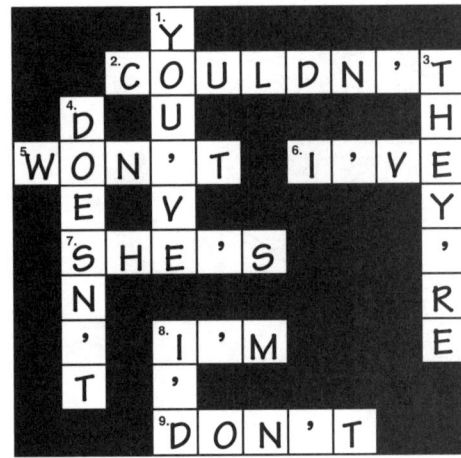

Page 59
1. 2—<u>O</u>ur, <u>D</u>r.
2. 1—<u>C</u>assie
3. 3—<u>A</u>llen, <u>S</u>mith, <u>I</u>ndiana
4. 2—<u>M</u>r., <u>P</u>urdy
5. 2—<u>E</u>veryone, <u>M</u>emorial
6. 3—<u>W</u>e, <u>B</u>oston, <u>M</u>assachusetts
7. 1—<u>T</u>hanksgiving
8. 3—<u>T</u>urn, <u>M</u>ain, <u>S</u>treet

Page 60
1. ☹ —Add commas after Sunnytown and July 10.
2. ☆ —No added commas necessary.
3. ✓ —Add commas after Lake and April 7 and Artie.
4. ✗ —Add comma after Mary.

Page 61
1. bronco
2. easel, ebony
3. farm, fast
4. jingle, jockey
5. picnic, pigsty

Pages 62–63
1. glossary
2. title page
3. table of contents
4. index

How Do You Foster Your Child's Interest in Learning?

In preparing this series, we surveyed scores of parents on this key question. Here are some of the best suggestions:

- Take weekly trips to the library to take out books, and attend special library events.

- Have lots of books around the house, especially on topics of specific interest to children.

- Read out loud nightly.

- Take turns reading to each other.

- Subscribe to age-appropriate magazines.

- Point out articles of interest in the newspaper or a magazine.

- Tell each other stories.

- Encourage children to write journal entries and short stories.

- Ask them to write letters and make cards for special occasions.

- Discuss all the things you do together.

- Limit TV time.

- Watch selected programs on TV together, like learning/educational channels.

- Provide project workbooks purchased at teacher supply stores.

- Supply lots of arts and crafts materials and encourage children to be creative.

- Encourage children to express themselves in a variety of ways.

- Take science and nature walks.

- Teach children to play challenging games such as chess.

- Provide educational board games.

- Supply lots of educational and recreational computer games.

- Discuss what children are learning and doing on a daily basis.

- Invite classmates and other friends over to your house for team homework assignments.

- Keep the learning experiences fun for children.

- Help children with their homework and class assignments.

- Take trips to museums and museum classes.

- Visits cities of historical interest.

- Takes trips to the ocean and other fun outdoor locations (fishing at lakes, mountain hikes).

Grades 1 & 2

- Visit the aquarium and zoo.

- Cook, bake, and measure ingredients.

- Encourage children to participate in sports.

- Listen to music, attend concerts, and encourage children to take music lessons.

- Be positive about books, trips, and other daily experiences.

- Take family walks.

- Let children be part of the family decision-making process.

- Sit down together to eat and talk.

- Give a lot of praise and positive reinforcement for your child's efforts.

- Review child's homework that has been returned by the teacher.

- Encourage children to use resources such as the dictionary, encyclopedia, thesaurus, and atlas.

- Plant a vegetable garden outdoors or in pots in your kitchen.

- Make each child in your family feel he or she is special.

- Don't allow children to give up, especially when it comes to learning and dealing with challenges.

- Instill a love of language; it will expose your child to a richer thought bank.

- Tell your children stories that share, not necessarily teach a lesson.

- Communicate your personal processes with your children.

- Don't talk about what your child did not do. Put more interest on what your child did do. Accept where your child is at, and praise his or her efforts.

- Express an interest in children's activities and schoolwork.

- Limit TV viewing time at home and foster good viewing habits.

- Work on enlarging children's vocabulary.

- Emphasize learning accomplishments, no matter how small.

- Go at their own pace; People learn at different rates.

- Challenge children to take risks.

- Encourage them to do their best, not be the best.